Best wishes,

Todd Jadot

Alaska's
Spectacular Aurora

Photography & Experiences by
Todd Salat

Published by
TODD SALAT SHOTS
645 G St., Suite 100, #798
Anchorage, Alaska 99501
USA

*To order additional copies of this book
please contact us at:*

Phone: (907) 250-4711
email: todd@aurorahunter.com

www.AuroraHunter.com

Graphic Design by Diane O'Neill
Illustrations by Clifton J. Derrick, III
Editing by Susan Dixon

Copyright © 2002 by Todd Salat
Library of Congress
Control Number: 2002094708
First Printing October, 2002
Second Printing January, 2005
ISBN: 1-57833-208-7
Printed in Seoul, Korea
First Edition

Distributed by
Todd Communications
203 W. 15th Ave. Suite 102
Anchorage, AK 99501-5128
Phone: (907) 274-8633
Fax: (907) 276-6858

All rights reserved.
No part of this publication may
be reproduced or used in any form or by any means:
graphic, electronic, or mechanical, including photocopying and
scanning, or by any information storage or retrieval system, in whole or in
part without the written permission of the publisher.

Dedicated
to Shay,
the love of my
life.

❦ Acknowledgements ❦

I would like to thank everyone who helped me take the leap of faith into becoming a full-time aurora hunter.

This includes the wonderful folks at **PhotoWright Laboratories** in Anchorage who process my film and do a SUPERB job of printing my limited edition prints, the core of my business. From the very beginning, their encouragement and professional quality service has been priceless.

Many thanks go out to **Denali Graphics & Frame** in Anchorage for doing <u>all</u> of my framing. If it were not for "D G & F" I would have spent many a clear night in my basement cutting mats and chopping frames instead of out shooting. They have been a critical member of the team.

Todd Communications (no relation) published my first photos in 1994 in their renowned Aurora Borealis Calendar. That was a major confidence booster. Today, they are the exclusive wholesale distributors for my line of Aurora Borealis Notecards and helped inspire me to pull this book together. Thank you, Flip Todd, and all of the staff at Todd Communications.

The music of **JoAnn & Monte** (Anchorage based) has led me down many inspirational paths and kept me entertained while on the road. They still can't believe I took their advice and quit my well-paying day job to become a fellow "artist." Hats off to the two of you!!

My parents thought it might happen some day, but I think they were a bit surprised with the news of my corporate resignation in 1996. As soon as possible I stuck a 30x40 inch aurora print in front of their eyes and they saw the light. They have been AVID supporters ever since. I am *so* thankful for this. Their support has always been "key, key, key."

I would like to dish out major kudos to the person to whom this book is dedicated: my wife, **Shay.** I had been a free-lance photographer for a year and a half when we met on a blind date in January of 1999. Since then she has helped me in many ways; as my muse, my inspiration, and my partner. Thank you for being you, Mrs. Salat.

Last, but not least, I would like to thank you, the viewer and reader of this book. Without your support we could not keep this lifestyle afloat. Therefore, you can count on the fact that we have a *very* deep appreciation for **YOU!**

ThanxSalat!!

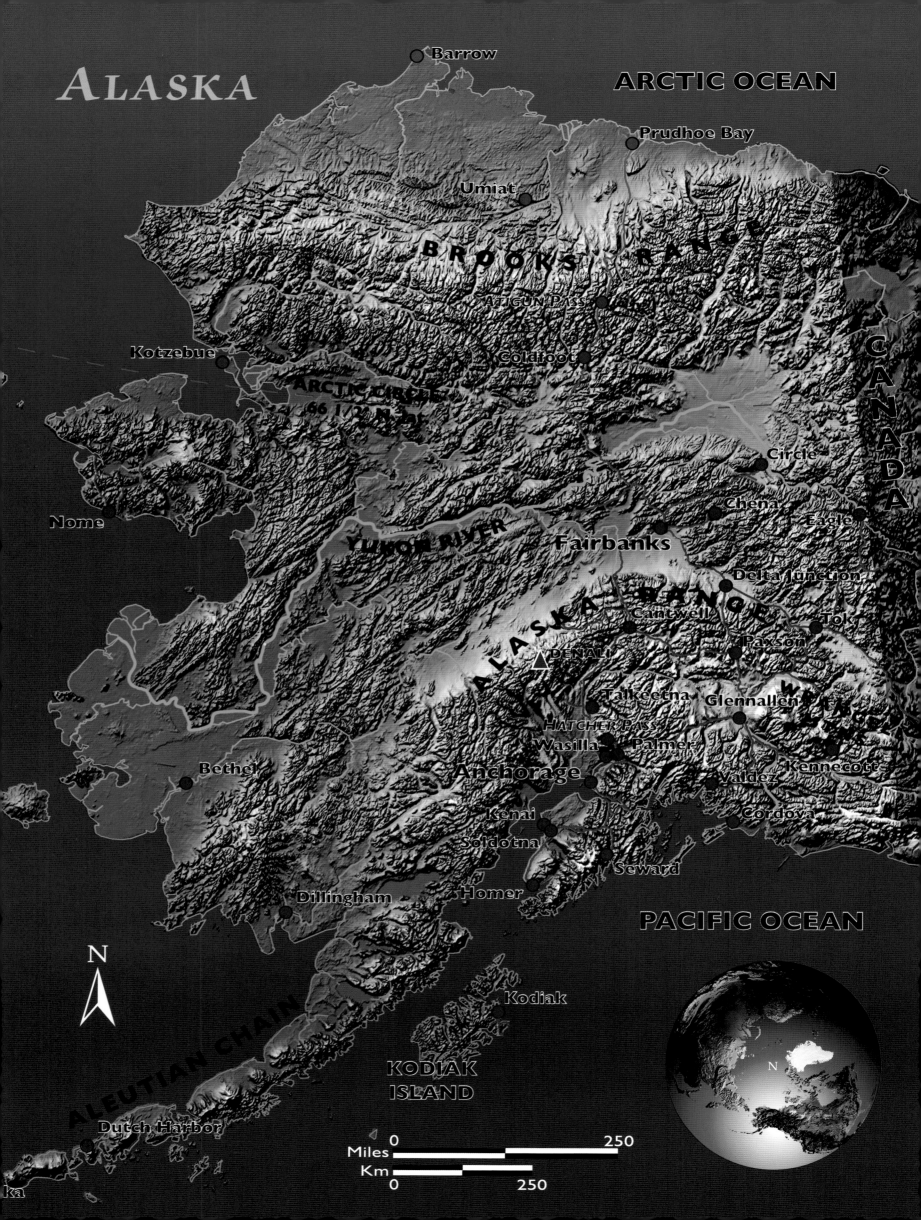

❧ CONTENTS ❧

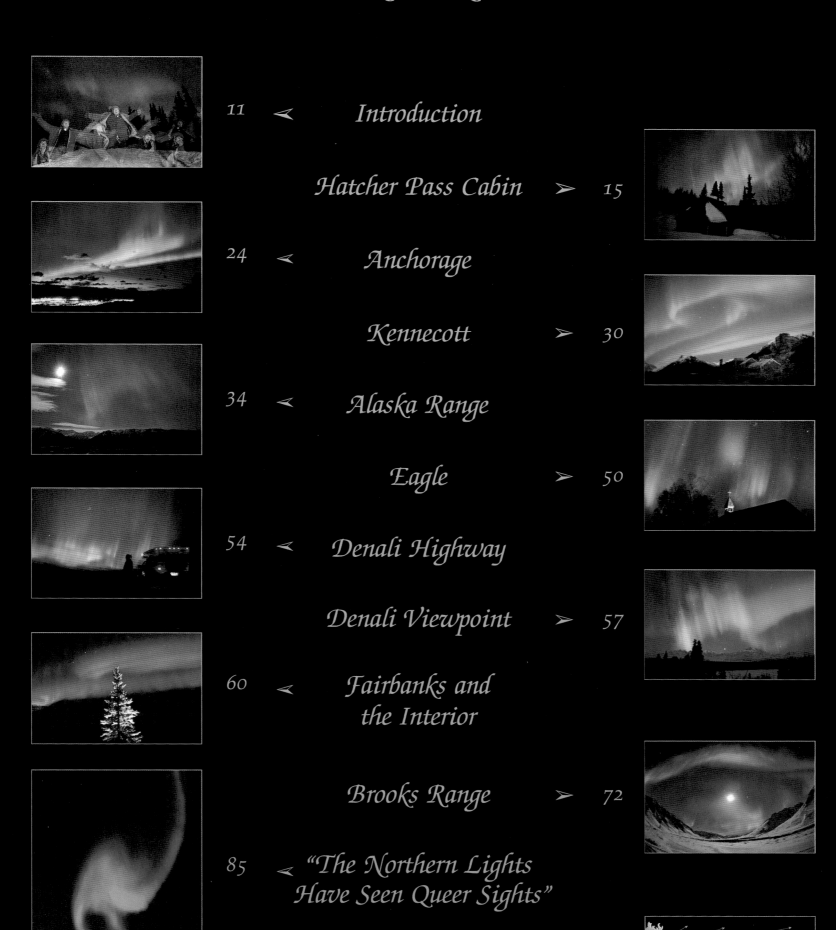

❧ Introduction ❧

Few things in nature can match the grandeur of the aurora. Generated by solar winds and able to illuminate our night skies with colored lights, this phenomenon is on a global scale and beyond.

Every auroral display is an unique experience, a moment ~ long or short ~ that leaves me thrilled to the bone. So much in fact that I feel compelled to preserve these peak moments of nature on film. I emphasize the word "preserve" because I do not believe it is possible to "capture" the aurora on film. It has way too much energy!

A photograph *is* worth a thousand words, but sometimes it can't completely convey a very important element, the *experience* of being there. Consequently, I like to write down the feelings and experiences associated with many of these photographs. This part is pure fun to me and, from day one, I have found sharing these very enjoyable and rewarding.

So put on your stocking cap and gloves
and please join me in these pages
*as we go **Aurora Hunting***
in the Great Land known
as Alaska.

MARCH 13-14, 1989

These dates would be remembered for one of the greatest magnetic storms of the 20th century. The sun had erupted a coronal mass ejection of charged particles and for two nights red auroras engulfed the Earth. People in parts of the world rarely treated to the aurora thought huge wildfires raged on the horizon. Reported UFO sightings were off the charts. It was the big one.

I stood in the foothills of the Rocky Mountains above Laramie, Wyoming with a bunch of fellow geology graduate students, drinks in hand, and watched. It was my first auroral experience. I remember temporarily putting our active scientific brains to rest, just staring at the ominous weird glow in the sky and saying "Wowwwww." At that moment I thanked my lucky stars. I had just landed a job as a geologist in Alaska, playground of the aurora borealis.

My First Aurora Photograph

The "Aurora Nights" Experience

It was April of 1990 and I had just completed my first winter in Anchorage, Alaska. Spring break-up had turned the "Great White North" into a humongous slush puddle. A buddy and I had spring fever so we decided to get out of town and air out the body and soul. We set up camp near Portage Glacier, fifty miles south of town, and started a big campfire. I had seen a few minor displays of northern lights that winter, but nothing to write home about. This particular night changed my attitude, and set me on a different course in life.

From over the mountains came a swirling mass of green light that made both my friend and I jump off our log seats and move away from the bright firelight. The aurora proceeded to fill the entire sky for what seemed like an eternity. It was my first experience with an all-night, all-sky auroral display.

Was it possible to photograph this incredible scene? I set up my little plastic tripod with a Pentax K-1000 manual camera, pointed it at the green lights and clicked open the shutter for about 20 seconds. I took two shots, put the camera away, then kicked back and enjoyed the show. When I got my film developed I was both surprised and excited to find that the northern lights could be recorded on just regular film, with nothing fancy. This photo was taken on that glorious evening and represents my first aurora shot and the beginning of my preoccupation with the **"Aurora Nights."**

✺ *Hatcher Pass Cabin* ✺

In 1993 I searched long and hard for a piece of land in Alaska that would take me to where my dreams were free to roam.   Eventually I found a half-built cabin in Hatcher Pass. It was eighty miles north of Anchorage ~ an adequate getaway distance ~ and the main beam of the cabin was aligned with the North Star. Perfect!

With the help of my dad and some friends we transformed the framed-out octagonal structure into an aurora viewer's delight.   By first snowfall, with cameras and tripods in hand, I was ready to cut my teeth on aurora photography.

"Moon Shadow"
is the most important
photo I've taken in my
entire life. In January of 1994
I was working enthusiastically
as a geologist in the corporate
world, but eagerly escaping to the
cabin every weekend to intensely
search the skies for the northern lights.

To me, the aurora in this photograph
looks like a question mark, as if asking:

What path in
life are you
going to choose **?**

*Two more years of soul-searching
provided a gut feeling,
and I resigned from my day job.*

The "Moon Shadow" Experience

It was a beautifully clear and cold Alaskan winter night in the middle of January. The moon was so bright you could read a newspaper by it. Some friends and I were hunting auroras at my Hatcher Pass cabin. We were concerned that if the lights did come out, the moon's brightness would overwhelm a good show...

We underestimated the power of the Aurora.

The first auroral arc was spotted on the distant northern horizon. Within an hour the arc had moved over us and headed south as it began to enter the peak moment known as the break-up stage. The sky came alive with spectacular white, pink and blue curtains of light. The main body drifted toward the moon. I turned my tripod, opened the shutter on my camera for several seconds and was fortunate enough to score the shot **"Moon Shadow."** I'll always remember that night when the northern lights were in the moon's face but still dominated the sky.

"Red Skies at Night"

"Arctic Rose"

"Purple Majesty"

One winter night I saw
"Five Live Bands"
at my Hatcher Pass cabin.

Film is a blank canvas . . .

. . . light is the paintbrush.

❧ Anchorage ❧

What can be said about aurora viewing under the big city lights of Anchorage? I've repeatedly heard that it's nearly impossible to see the northern lights from the city because of the light pollution. I jotted this down as I stood there, in the city, watching a beautiful greenish-white curtain of light gracefully dance across the high northern sky.

If I could convey one message to anyone in a northern city during the dark hours of the night, it would be to *please* "look up." Whether you're inside or outside, use your arms and hands to shield your eyes from those annoying streetlights, and focus into the northern sky.

No city light can stop this kind of show.

This holiday display was viewed to the northwest from Bootleggers Cove near downtown Anchorage.

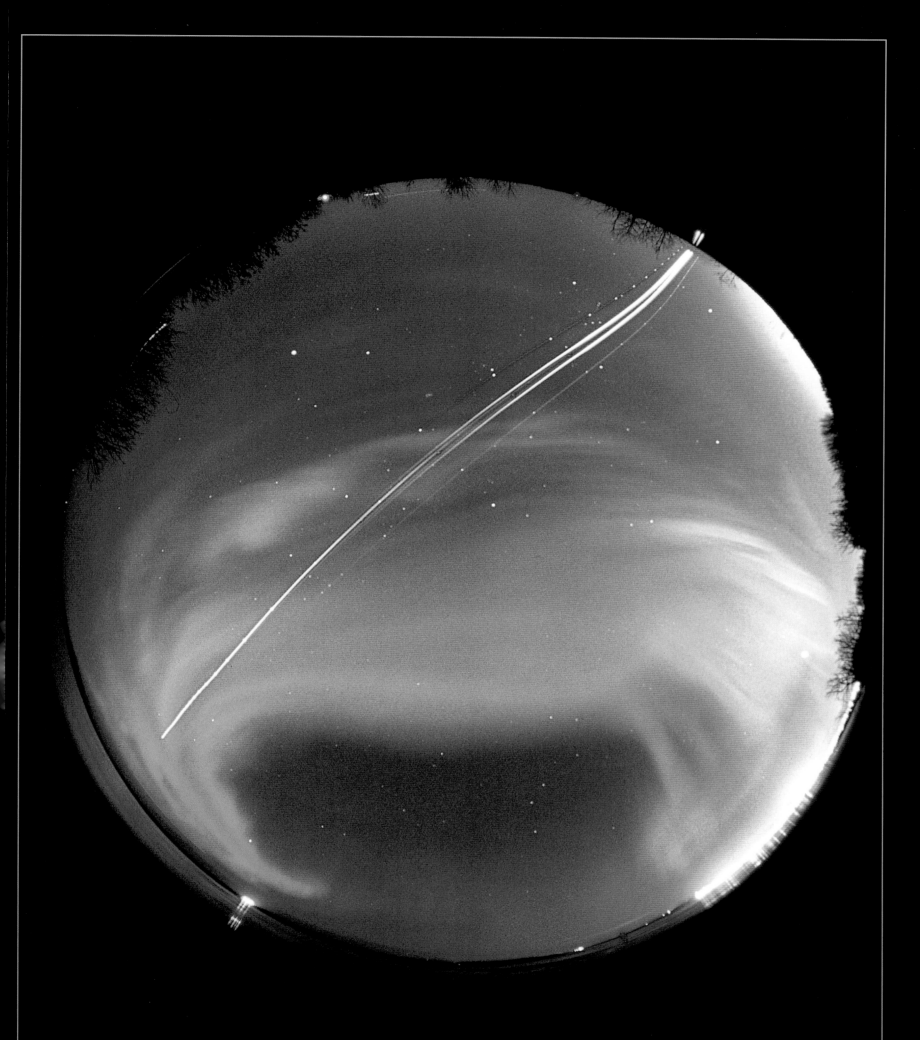

A 7.5mm all-sky fisheye lens takes in the whole scene from a bluff overlooking Cook Inlet near Earthquake Park. The light trails are from an airplane departing the nearby Ted Stevens Anchorage International Airport, deafening me during this half-minute exposure.

The "Anchorage Aglow" Experience

"There's darkness at the end of the tunnel." That's my motto when August hits Alaska and the long light-enriched summer days (daze) are starting to fade quietly into the sunset. For three full months, May, June and July, it just does *not* get very dark. August, however, leaves no doubt that the auroras are back for another season.

I made the rounds to my favorite local Anchorage viewing spots like Pt. Woronzof and Arctic Valley, but it was from the Flattop overlook that I got the view I really wanted. On August 19th, at the stroke of midnight, two bands converged over the city as the lower pink border announced the peak moment of this auroral break-up. A zillion little shards of light rippled swiftly across the distant band, while the frontal arc sent colossal rays high into the sky.

Nearby puffs of clouds were illuminated by the city lights below. Even at this hour the orange glow in the northern distance was evidence that the sun was not very far over the hill. But it was dark ~ beautiful Alaskan darkness glowing with colors: orange and blue, pink and green. Glowing inside and outside, this is *"Anchorage Aglow."*

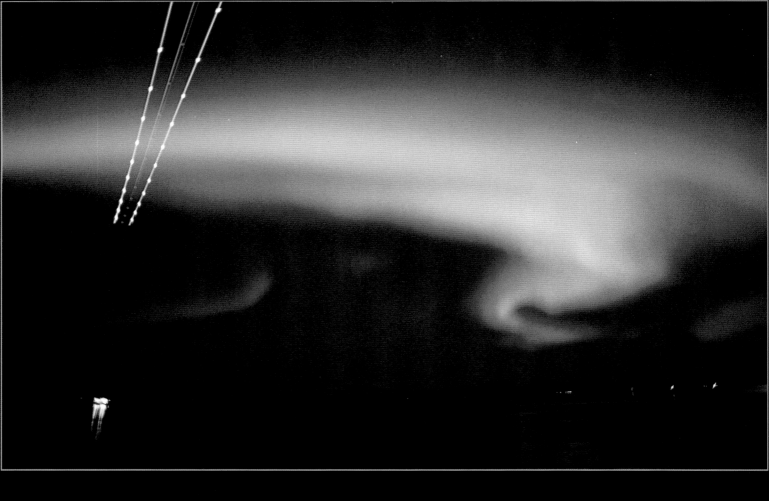

These three Anchorage photographs were taken from Pt. Woronzof at the western end of the (appropriately named) Northern Lights Boulevard. The auroras are reflecting off the calm Pacific waters of Cook Inlet.

Photo on right: **"Legendary Lady"** shows Mt. Susitna, known as the "Sleeping Lady."

❧ *Kennecott* ❧

Most people I speak with who have visited the Kennecott area in the heart of the Wrangell Mountains have a sparkle in their eye when recounting their experiences. It is *very* magical country.

The "Kennecott Treasures" Experience

This year's fall project was to explore the Kennecott area in the Wrangell/St. Elias National Park and Preserve. Built in the early 1900's near a huge copper deposit, the Kennecott mill town has partially withstood the test of time, and partially weathered into a captivating ghost mine. The artistic appeal had me hooked and left me with an uncontrollable desire to photograph the aurora borealis dancing over the rustic red structures.

On a September backpacking trip I didn't get lucky with the aurora, so the first of October found me once again driving down McCarthy Road, a notorious sixty-mile stretch of gravel that runs from Chitina to the McCarthy area. I parked my rig at the Tram Station and faced a dilemma. After crossing the narrow footbridge over the Kennicott River (note spelling difference), how was I going to get two weeks worth of food and gear, probably a 150 pound load, up the five-mile gravel road to Kennecott? At this point I struck a great fortune ~ the operator of the Tram Station offered me his Subaru, which was on the Kennecott side of the river. Yes! Thanks Randy! The vehicle also served as a huge bear-proof container to store my food in.

I threw my sleeping pad in the back and that Subaru became my home away from home. I was on a treasure hunt.

On that very first lucky night, the treasure was uncovered. I drove up the hill to the mill, found my favorite northward viewing angle about 100 yards from the mill buildings and set up both tripods and cameras. The sky was clear, and just as I finished up a gourmet meal of noodles, a green aurora band materialized out of thin air. It got brighter and brighter . . . faded . . . then returned with a few of its friends. Soon four bands were dancing through the Big Dipper. A full moon in the sky lit up the snow on nearby Donoho Peak and the surrounding mountains, but the red buildings were just too dark to catch the moonlight.

"Kennecott Treasures"

*I thought the mill site would need extra illumination,
so I had thrown in my million candlepower 12-volt spotlight.*

I plugged the spotlight into the Soob's cigarette lighter, and after locking the camera shutter open, I grabbed the spotlight and painted the buildings with a beam of light for several seconds. I experimented with many different beaming techniques and exposure times. The reward was the experience and one keeper, **"Kennecott Treasures."**

To the west of Kennecott the aurora erupts from behind the 16,390 foot moonlit Mt. Blackburn in the Wrangell Mountains. Mt. Donoho is on the right.

This photo was taken five miles beyond the mill site in early October, a few days after the spotlit Kennecott shots were taken. The trail follows the edge of Root Glacier until it hits the "Stairway," the moonlit glacier located at the end of this valley.

❧ *Alaska Range* ❧

The Alaska Range is at a prime latitude (63° N) for aurora hunting. Three different highways transect the range, making it easily accessible in winter. I have had some of my most memorable experiences in these mountains.

The "Slice of Heaven" Experience
(overleaf)

I was aurora hunting for a week and had not even taken the cap off my camera lens. It was the full moon phase in early November and I was camping and cruising through the Alaska Range on the Richardson Highway. This is a quiet and wonderfully desolate stretch of road between Paxson and Delta Junction, especially at night.

During the first three evenings the sky was clear but devoid of auroral activity ~ I finished all of my photo biz projects. The next four nights were completely shrouded in clouds ~ I accomplished a lot of reading. I thought about writing a book on aurora hunting and wanted to give it the title "Waiting . . . and Waiting . . . ." I noticed my thoughts were starting to repeat themselves in a peculiar manner and I couldn't help but recognize the symptoms: I was getting a slight case of "camper fever."

I remember it well . . . Around 4 am on the seventh night I plugged in my anthem, a rock 'n roll song called *Shine* by Collective Soul. By the time the main chorus rang out "Heaven let your light shine on me," I was out in the snow doing the "Dances with Wolves" jig. After about a half an hour of this exercise I decided to break camp and just drive. I lowered the pop-up camper and put the truck into gear. Before I knew it, the clouds began to part ~ and blammo, the aurora came shining through. I was ecstatic! Thank you, Collective Soul (and beyond).

Later, as I recounted this whole experience in detail on the phone to my parents, I heard my mother softly whisper, "Wow, sounds like a **'Slice of Heaven'**." To me, in three words, that describes it all. Thanxsalat for the title, Mom.

I will forever refer to the Alaska Range transected by the Richardson Highway as **"Slice of Heaven"** *country.*

Beginning on November 7, 1998, I was treated to three nights of unbelievable aurora action that has led me to call this a "Quintessential Auroral Experience." I cannot deny that I felt spiritually enlightened by these displays.

Photo titles for the following pages:
"Slice of Heaven"
"Rainbow Ridge"
"Sky Highways"
"The Phoenix"
"Angel"
"Butterfly"
"Dipper in Hand"

"Divine Light"

This photograph represents more of a feeling than an experience to me. As I lie there on my back in the snow, looking straight up at one of Mother Nature's finest displays of beauty, the aurora borealis, I am captivated by a feeling.

It's energy of some sort ~ and connecting with it is an almost indescribable euphoria. I know all of you have probably had that feeling before. If it's been a while, it is right outside the door; a beautiful sunset, a full moon, a sky full of stars, the howl of a lone wolf, the northern lights . . .

The feeling is so simple and pure that it completely clears my mind of the daily noise. It's very therapeutic and just plain fun! It definitely charges my battery and makes me want to share this feeling with everyone. There's just something about looking at the **"Divine Light."**

"Onlooker"

I stood on this knoll for four
nights waiting and watching for
the elusive springtime aurora.
I was in the Alaska Range near the
Parks Highway and in just a few
days it would be May. This was
the last aurora hunt of the season.

❦ Eagle ❦

Eagle, Alaska is a quaint and welcoming community to the traveler. No one may know your name, but the sense of belonging is comforting. It's one of those special places that as soon as you leave it, you miss it, and start planning a return trip.

The "Heaven & Earth" Experience

Every September I like to start off the aurora season with a bang and travel somewhere remote. This fall I had a new travel partner, Shay, who later became my wife. We pulled out the road atlas and spotted a dot on the map that we had never visited ~ Eagle, Alaska.

Shay has the spirit!

Veering north off of the Alcan, we bounced our way up the Taylor Highway, stopping for a rest in the town of Chicken. Ninety-five miles of gravel later, the road abruptly stopped at Eagle, right on the edge of the mighty Yukon River. We stepped out, took a deep breath of cool autumn air and instantly felt refreshed.

We started exploring every avenue and eventually came to the old St. Paul's Church. Built in 1901 during the gold rush era, the small one-story building glows with turn-of-the-century history as it sits on the bank of the swift and mesmerizing river. A big ol' birch tree, probably as old as the church, has grown healthy and tall next to it. I knew right then and there that come nightfall I would search here for that spiritual experience.

Around 10 pm the first green arc appeared on the northern horizon. Soon tall, colorful rays decorated the sky like a huge pane of stained glass. I began photographing the aurora from all angles while illuminating the church with every creative lighting technique I could think of.

During one peak moment I clicked the shutter open on my tripod-mounted camera, sprinted in my clunky boots to the backside of the church, and "poofed" the little steeple with a hand-held flash unit, then ran back and clicked off the camera. In the half-minute that elapsed, the film recorded the glory that I could see, and intensified the wonderfully deep purples that went beyond what my eyes could detect. I believe all that light and color is there; we just can't see it all!

"Heaven & Earth"

Here on earth we have trees, churches and rivers.
Up there in the sky is heavenly beauty,
some we can see and some we cannot,
but deep down inside we know it's there.

❦ *Denali Highway* ❦

This 136-mile "highway" is mostly gravel and connects Paxson with Cantwell as it sidles along the glaciated southern flank of the Alaska Range. It used to be the only route to Denali National Park before the Parks Highway was built. Nowadays, it serves as a scenic getaway ~ a place to get lost without ever really losing your way.

The "Big Red" Experience

This autumn was devoted to hunting **"Big Red"** ~ the elusive red aurora. My wife and I were on our third night of a road trip as we blissfully puttered our way eastward across the Denali Highway. It was September 22, the autumnal equinox, and the stars hung like jewels in the night against pitch dark skies. We felt one with Alaska as we searched for a sign of the northern lights.

At 11 pm a faint, almost undetectable band appeared over the northeastern horizon. That was warning enough as we readied the tripods and locked and loaded the cameras. It was a good thing we were prepared because when the aurora borealis surged westward it took only minutes for them to consume the entire northern sky.

The band quickly expanded into columns of crimson red that stretched upward toward the zenith. The aurora peaked in front of us as the V-shaped stars of the Hyades (the head of Taurus the Bull) and the seven sisters of the Pleiades cluster twinkled through the powerful luminescence. The bright planet of Saturn shone like a beacon (left side of photo). We stood spellbound, wondering if we could believe our eyes. This was the real thing, RED as could be.

"Big Red"

A successful aurora hunt:
The right place, the right time,
and lots of LUCK!

❧ Denali Viewpoint ❧

Located at milepost 135 on the Parks Highway, this viewpoint offers an outstanding view of Mt. McKinley, more affectionately known as Denali. The northwesterly viewing angle is critical for catching a glimpse of two positive energy sources in the same frame, Denali and the aurora borealis. This earth/sky combo can really put on a show.

The "Denali Dance" Experience

It was just past midnight on a March evening and I was camped at milepost 135 on the Parks Highway. I was on a serious aurora hunt and it was the 30th night this winter that I had spent with Denali in my sights. My inverted schedule began like all the rest; I awoke at 7:30 pm, did a few stretches to get rid of the camper kinks, cooked up breakfast around 8 pm, then took a brisk walk. I was in a good space as I focused both my camera/tripod setups on Denali, then settled into the front seat of my truck.

It was -10° F with optimal conditions; calm and clear skies with a near full moon lighting up the snowscape. The skies had been completely devoid of any auroral activity for several nights and I had passed the time just stargazing. I decided that maybe I was wanting this shot too much, so I just let it go . . .

"If it happens, it happens," I thought to myself. That night it happened.

I have developed a sleep-with-one-eye-open technique for aurora hunting. After sitting in the front of my warm truck for a couple of hours, that's exactly what I was doing ~ snoozin! All of a sudden my one alert eye screamed at my other eye, "Wake Up!" and when I did I gasped. Huge, tall curtains of green and pink light were dancing right over Denali! I flew out of my truck and in one gigantic bound I was at my cameras. I just started bracketing different exposures: two seconds, four seconds, eight seconds . . . This was supposed to be relaxing, but talk about an adrenaline rush!

The curtains were climbing right out of the Alaska Range and performing a mix of tap dance and ballet ~ it was absolutely extraordinary! Within ten minutes the peak moment was over and the aurora gracefully bowed and faded into the northern sky. I stood there whispering, "Don't leave . . . come back . . . ." Oh, so bittersweet.

And so it was, the highest mountain on this continent and what I believe to be nature's most magical phenomenon, the aurora borealis, getting together for one brief interlude, an exquisite high energy dance ~ the **"Denali Dance."**

This photo was taken looking northwest across the frozen Chulitna River braid plain at an elevation of 600 feet. About forty miles away and rising almost four miles is Denali, meaning "The High One" in the native Athabaskan language. The prominent peak is known as the "South Peak" of Denali and is the highest point in North America at 20,320 feet. Although these auroras appear to touch the ground they are 200-400 miles away and about 50-300 miles high.

The "Goddess of Dawn" Experience

The aurora forecast was for quiet skies. I thought about staying home, but the auroras are not always predictable and the call of the wild is unrelenting. It was late January, the heart, depth and soul of winter in Alaska. When I asked my wife what kind of new aurora shot she would like to see, she replied, "How about some red auroras over Denali?" Whew! The challenge was on.

I found myself at milepost 135 on the Parks Highway. Four years earlier I had obsessed for thirty nights at this location trying to get a "hero shot." This time it happened on the third night, right at the crack of dawn.

The bright planet of Jupiter was setting over the Ruth Glacier as the early morning alpenglow illuminated Denali. I couldn't believe my eyes when, out of the deep blue skies, a towering curtain of red and teal northern lights developed in the twilight's first gleaming. Castor and Pollux, the twin stars of Gemini, twinkled in the candy-like colors above the tall spruce trees while the five-star pattern of Auriga the Charioteer graced the other side of the sky.

This was a precious moment as the aurora, "Goddess of Dawn," unveiled her otherworldly artistry.

In Roman mythology, Aurora, the goddess of dawn, opened the gates of heaven every morning for Apollo, the sun god. In the late 17th century, the Italian astronomer Galileo used the name "Aurora" to explain the luminous glow in the nighttime sky. He believed that the dancing lights were caused by sunlight reflecting off the atmosphere during the coming dawn. This theory is no longer accepted but the name *aurora* lives on.

✒ Fairbanks and the Interior ✒

The Interior of Alaska might as well be called "Auroraville." It couldn't be more perfectly positioned for northern lights viewing. Defined as everything north of the Alaska Range and south of the Brooks Range, the Interior sits directly under the auroral oval, the most common zone for activity. On any clear and dark night (which eliminates summer) the chances of at least seeing a bit of an aurora display are astronomically high.

Fairbanks is the central hub of the Interior. From there, all roads and rivers lead to potential aurora viewing opportunities.

View from Ester Dome, Fairbanks (March)

Candlelit cabin near Chena Hot Springs (February)

*Auroras coming over the Alaska Range and **"Into the Interior"** (November)*

The snowcat tour to the top of the hill at Chena Hot Springs (February)

"Circle over Circle" *from Eagle Summit on the Steese Highway (January)*
Circle Hot Springs provided much needed relief after this -40° F night.

Camping at the end of the Elliot Highway (October)
Manley Hot Springs was just down the road after the fire went out!

The "Great Bear" Experience

It was early September in the Interior ~ time to get out and eat the berries and look for those first auroras of the season. I parked along Chena Hot Springs Road near the Granite Tors Trail, loaded up the backpack and started hiking. While raiding the first berry patch I came to, I thought of what a ranger had said to me back in Fairbanks, "Don't worry buddy, the bears are full of salmon this time of year." I plodded on. Several miles later I came across an inviting campsite next to a big tor (a granite outcrop), pitched my tent and kicked back to enjoy the sunset. The stars started popping out above me as the final vestiges of daylight were fading over the northwestern horizon.

All of a sudden I saw a funny movement in the clouds above the sunset. I thought it was my imagination until a green spike shot out of the amber glow and removed all doubt; it was time for the northern lights to take over the show. I love it when they do that! The nearest band did a little flip-curl for the camera and headed into the Dipper.

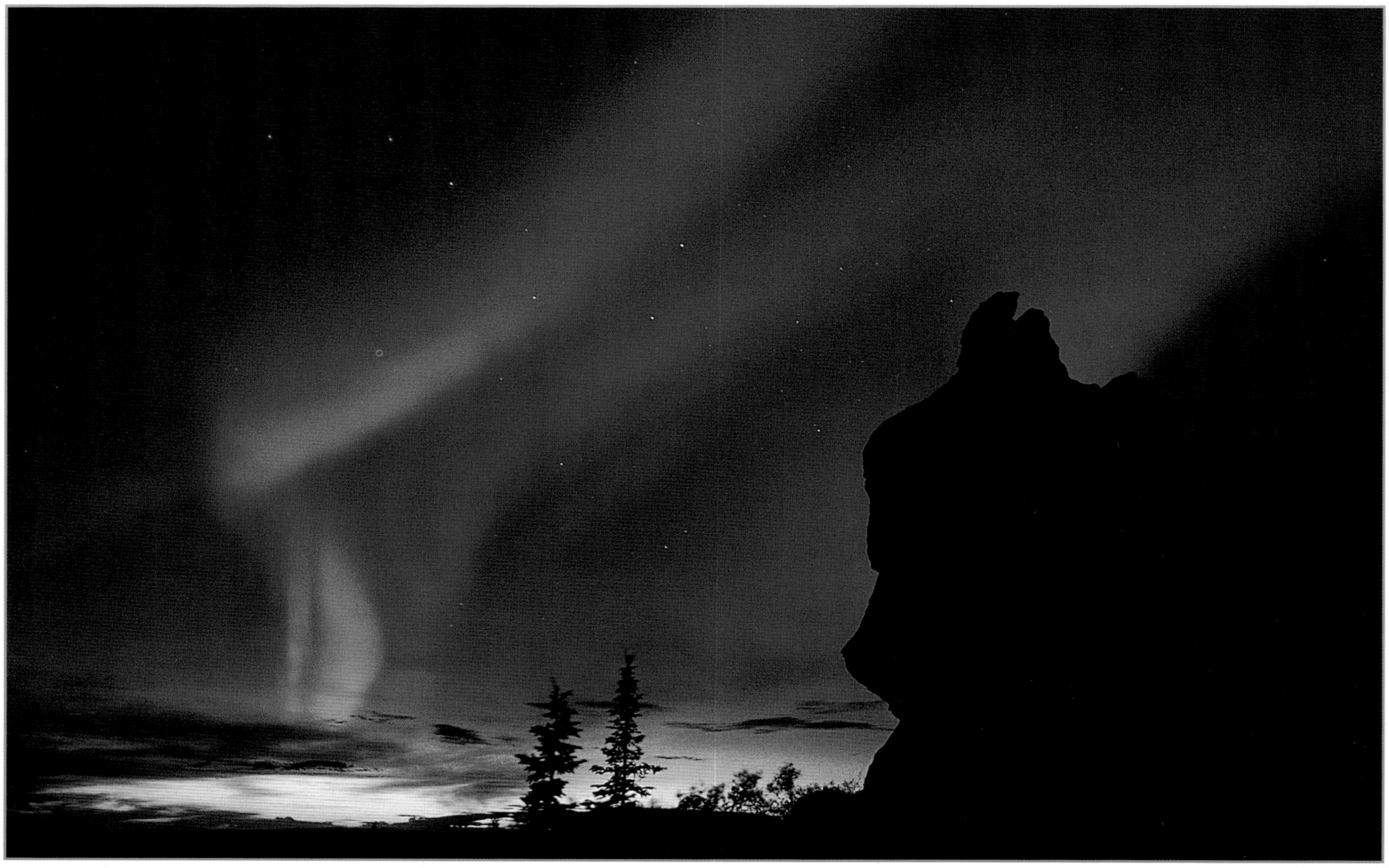

The Big Dipper is actually the tail and rear-end of the constellation Ursa Major (Great Bear). I noticed that the silhouetted profile of the granite tor I was camped under looked just like the head of a bear. Some say Pooh bear!

The auroras danced the night away among my **"Great Bear"** friends, and I am happy to report that no bears of the fuzzy variety decided to join me in the fun that night.

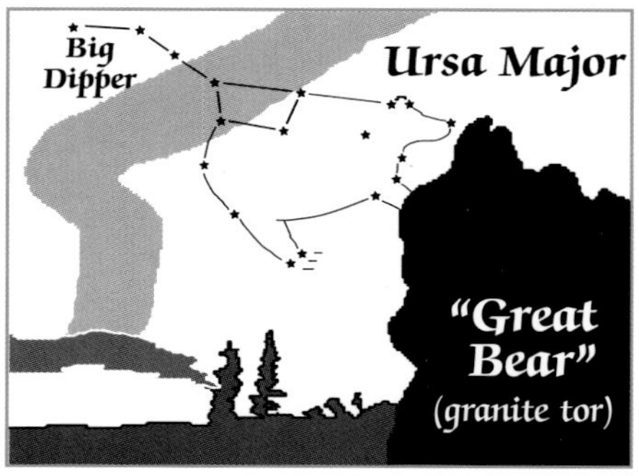

The "Alaska Magic" Experience

It was a frosty September night and I was enjoying my birthday while aurora hunting on top of Murphy Dome, just west of Fairbanks. At midnight, in the pitch dark new moon (i.e., no moon) skies, I got my birthday present ~ a beautiful emerald green aurora.

Usually, I like to photograph auroras on moonlit nights so a foreground shows up in the picture, but tonight I knew I'd have to create my own. I searched for the best looking spruce tree I could find (not always an easy thing to do in Alaska, especially at night) and found a big ol' Christmas tree. I lined it up with the Big Dipper and just as the aurora started to really glow I locked open the camera shutter, scrambled and tumbled my way behind the tree, and backlit it with two "poofs" from my hand-held flash unit. Ta-Dum! That was my contribution to **"Alaska Magic."** You'll have to ask Mother Nature how she added *her* secret ingredient.

GREEK MYTHOLOGY NOTE: Bears really don't have much for tails, so the tail in Ursa Major (the handle of the Big Dipper) had to be explained. One myth states that Zeus lifted the bears (Ursa Major and Minor) into the sky, which stretched their tails. My favorite one tells the story of how Hercules had to rid a country of two troublesome bears, so he grabbed them by the tails, swung them around his head and flung them into the sky. That would definitely explain the stretched tails! Native American mythology recognizes the three stars in the tail area as three hunters following the main body of the Great Bear.

The
"Lady and Dakaben"
Experience

February is typically a deep freeze month when I expect to be lone wolfin' it on my aurora hunts. But this winter I had the good fortune of being invited to do some cabin-sitting at "Dakaben," a wonderful retreat owned by friends on Cleary Summit, twenty miles north of Fairbanks. With the modern conveniences of home (like heat!) I was able to convince my wife to fly up from Anchorage and keep me company.

I had just driven down to Fairbanks and picked up Shay at the airport when we were caught off guard and off post. A shoot of green light had suddenly sprouted in the rich black sky. "Yeouza!" It was only 8 pm!

You've got to watch those Interior auroras. They're sneaky and fast!

We roared out of town and made it to Dakaben just as the auroras started ripping. We frantically ran around grabbing gloves, hats, boots, lenses, tripods, headlamps, bumping into each other ~ no time to spare! The auroras started to curl overhead as I raced below "da cabin" and began taking shots. I saw Shay staring from the deck as though she couldn't move. Perfect! She steadied herself against a deck post, looked up and waited for those words she knew were coming, "Okay, stand perfectly still for 12 seconds!" Click. One thousand one, one thousand two, one thousand three . . . . . . one thousand twelve. Click.

Thanks Michael, Pat, and George for the naming and the use of Dakaben and Daudderkaben.

"Dakaben"

Auroras over the cabin, Cleary Summit, twenty miles north of Fairbanks (February)

"Daudderkaben"

Auroras over "da other cabin"

Way up north . . . Way up north . . . North to Alaska,
[We're] going north, the rush is on!

With the northern lights a runnin' wild
in the land of the midnight sun . . .

[We] crossed the majestic mountains
to the valleys far below . . .

(from the song "North to Alaska" performed by Johnny Horton)

North of Fairbanks the highway names change quickly from the Steese to the Elliott and finally to the Dalton (also known as the Haul Road). This 414-mile gravel road follows the Trans Alaska Pipeline all the way to Prudhoe Bay/Deadhorse. It is also the only road to cross over the Brooks Range, the northernmost mountain range in Alaska. This is the next destination . . .

The auroras
wait for no one!

While road-tripping to the Brooks Range on my first aurora hunt into the area, it was very difficult making northward progress ~ the auroras were *everywhere!*

The photo to the right and the shot of the semi truck lights on the next page were taken at the top of a treacherous Haul Road hill dubbed the "Beaver Slide" by truck drivers.

LET'S
GO TO THE
BROOKS RANGE

❧ Brooks Range ☙

I discovered my passion for the Brooks Range while working as an exploration geologist, banging on outcrops with a rock hammer and chewing on the chips to guesstimate grain size (yup, gritty). Company-provided helicopter support gave me an aerial perspective and an appreciation for the immensity of these mountains.

These days, with only truck/camper support, I'm more focused on the light hitting the rock strata than on the economic potential they may hold. The combination of remoteness, fascinating geology and clarity of light, makes this one of my favorite places on earth ~ and the aurora hunting is hard to beat.

The "Valley of Light" Experience

I dropped my truck into first gear as I slowly chugged up the semi-narrow and winding road to Atigun Pass. It looked like avalanche country. Several minutes later I was standing on the continental divide in the Brooks Range of northern Alaska.

Gazing north into the moonlit October night my sense of awe grew strong as I took in the entire grandeur of the valley far below. It was a perfect U-shape, carved out by an alpine glacier several millennia before. I slowly descended into it and camped out for a week.

Every clear evening I celebrated the moonrise as it illuminated the snow-covered topography. Sometimes the aurora would join me in this escapade. To me, it was photogenic paradise.

One night, a fast-moving arc appeared from the south as the full moon centered itself in the valley. Only my widest angle lens (16mm fisheye) could get the full 180° scene into the viewfinder.

"Valley of Light"

The natural symmetry of the moment was exhilarating.
I can easily remember that wonderful feeling of standing
there, so small, in the enormity of the "Valley of Light."

The "St★rdust" Experience
Romantic, magical, ethereal (heavenly) ~ the definition of "Stardust"

After spending a wonderful week camping in the Brooks Range I started to run low on precious fuel and decided it was time to head homeward. At the base of Atigun Pass, I paused for a couple of hours. I was happy I did when at 5:55 am, just before dawn, a huge auroral connection was made. I broke away from the confines of the road, slid down a hill into a bowl where a pack of wolves had left their trail, and started to compose.

A powerful glow began to emanate from the mountains to the east. With uncanny speed, pink and turquoise blue curtains of light came shooting up and over my head.

I spun my tripod, gazed upwards and there it was:

Stardust
speckled snow,
stratified rock layers,
a brilliant moon,
a star field of
constellations ~
Gemini, Auriga,
the Pleiades, Taurus ~
and the aurora.

Heavenly blue,
romantic red and
magical magenta
cascaded down all
around me.

This is the stuff that **"Stardust"** is made of.

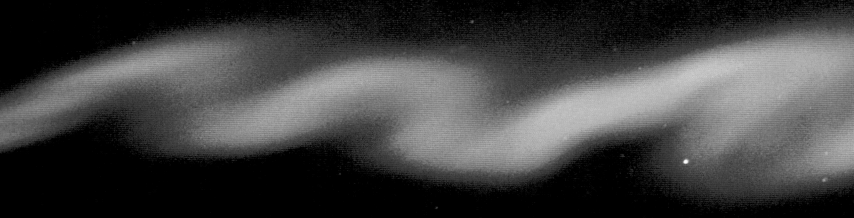

I call them "eddies of light" ~
technically they are called "curls."

Like water flowing around a boulder in a stream, these eddies of light are turbulence on a grand scale. I have few photographs of them. Not only are they rarely this well defined, but their fluid-like flow is so mesmerizing, I just have to stop and watch.

"The Great Unknown"

❧ "The Northern Lights ❧ Have Seen Queer Sights"

This quote from the popular Robert Service poem, *The Cremation of Sam McGee*, rings in my head every time something strange shows up in the sky or on film.

"Baboon"

I have seen many bizarre aurora shapes as they pulsated around the sky, but I still never know what the film will show compared to what meets the eye. I collect my film at the end of night when the aurora and I are spent, and take them to the lab excited as a young lad opening a Christmas present.

"Sky Dog"

Here are several shots from my "faces and shapes" collection. Feel free to name or rename them based on what *you* see.

The "Hypnotized" Experience

A
small
group of
friends and I
were hangin' outside my
Hatcher Pass cabin enjoying
another beautiful winter weekend.
A full moon hung in the sky, brilliantly
illuminating everything. Nighttime navigation
did not even require a headlamp. Earlier, the auroras
had been explosive, but for now we wondered if they
had gone to bed for the night.

I was tending the woodstove when
I heard a holler. With very little warning,
the aurora came whipping in from the northwest.
I scrambled to my 'pods and started clicking away
exposures. I glanced down the road and there stood
my friend, "Duck." He looked awe-struck, or was he just
frozen in an upright position? I yelled, "Don't move a muscle, Duck!"
and started stalking toward him, taking a couple of shots along the way.

As I approached, I lowered my tripod and pointed the camera straight up
at him. As the aurora curled overhead I clicked open the camera shutter for a solid
six seconds. For a moment, it looked like Duck was **"Hypnotized"** by what I'd like to
think is an auroral angel (albeit a kind of scary looking one). I see the eyes, the face, the
mouth and the flowing hair. Others say they see a snake or a dolphin.

*It seems that no two people see the same thing in a live display or a still
photograph of the aurora, so let your imaginations flow . . .
The sky is the limit!*

❦ *Science* ❦

How the Auroras Form

The auroras form when charged protons and electrons emitted from the sun (solar wind) penetrate the earth's magnetic shield and collide with atoms and molecules in our atmosphere. These collisions result in countless little bursts of light, called photons, which make up the aurora. Collisions with oxygen produce red and green auroras, while nitrogen produces the pink and purple colors. This reaction encircles the polar regions of the earth and occurs at an altitude of 40-400 miles in a zone called the "Auroral Oval."

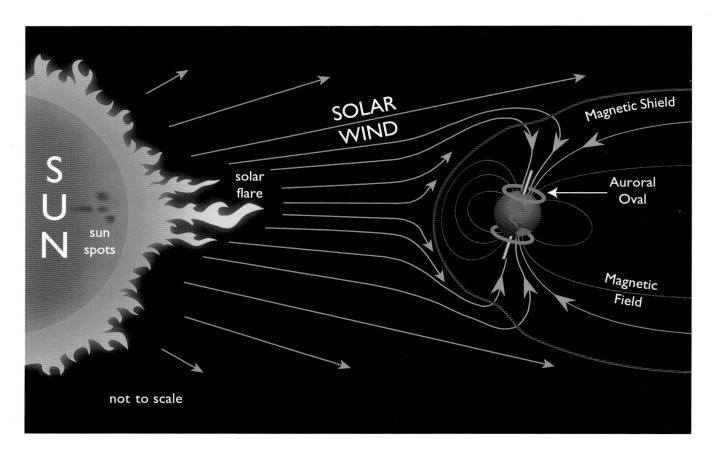

Where and When

The auroras most commonly occur between 60°-75° latitude, but during great magnetic storms the auroral oval expands equatorially and can reach 30° latitude or further. In the northern hemisphere they are called the *aurora borealis* (northern lights) and in the southern hemisphere *aurora australis* (southern lights).

An auroral display might be observed any night from dusk until dawn as long as it is dark, which excludes Alaskan summer nights. The best time to view them is between midnight and 2 am. There is an 11-year solar cycle (on average) that controls the tempo of the auroras. The most recent peak in the cycle occurred in 2000-2001.

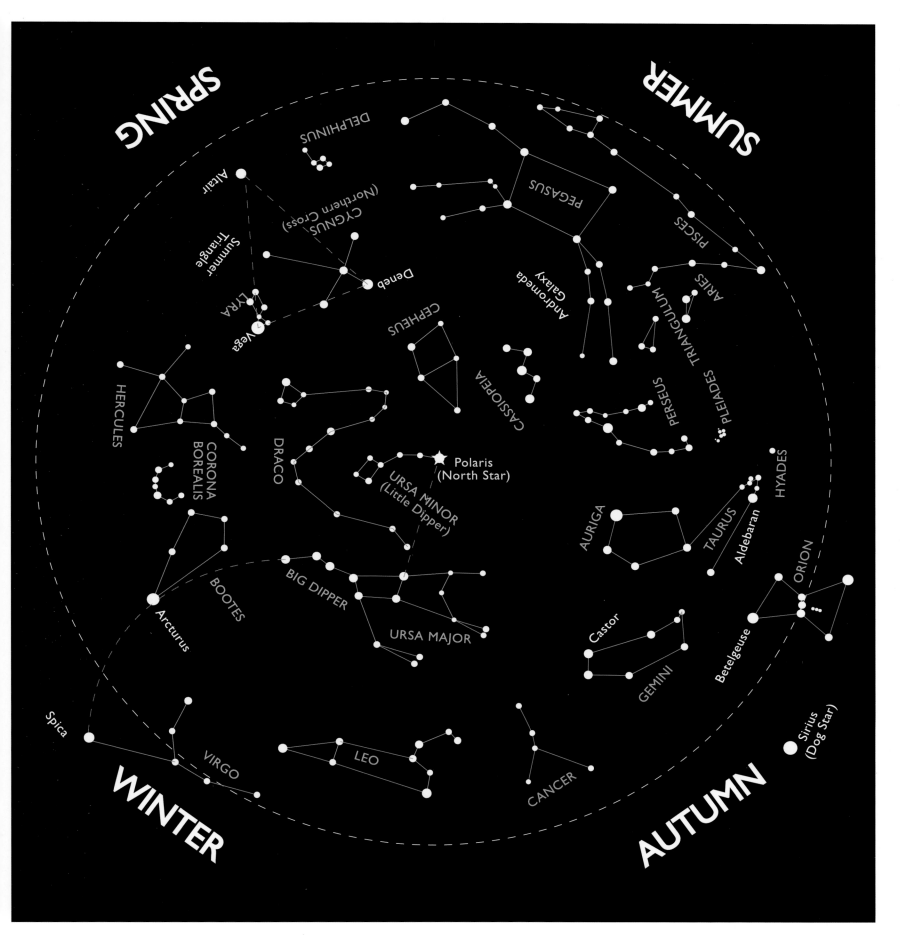

Star Chart for the Northern Hemisphere

To orient yourself with the stars, face north and rotate the chart until the current season shows at the bottom. The constellations at the bottom of the chart will be in the northern sky, while the stars at the top of the chart will be to the south. This is based on midnight stargazing. As the night progresses, the stars will appear to rotate counter-clockwise due to the rotation of the earth.

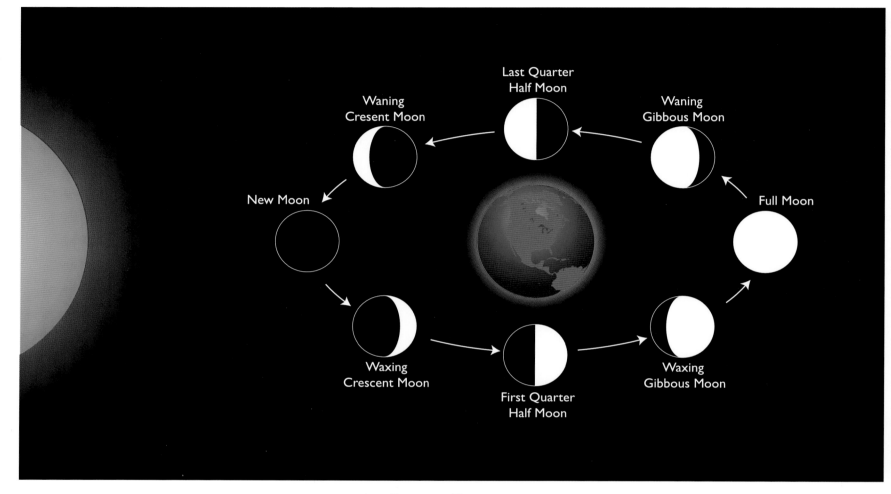

LUNAR PHASES
(as viewed from earth)

Phases of the moon as seen from earth during one lunar month: a 29 ¼ day revolution around the earth. When the moon is in the shape of a "D" it is developing (waxing) into a full moon. When it is in the shape of a "C" it is constricting (waning) into a new moon (i.e., no moon).

Statement of Authenticity

IN NO WAY HAVE ANY OF THE PHOTOGRAPHS IN THIS BOOK BEEN ENHANCED OR MANIPULATED BY COMPUTERS OR COLOR FILTERS.

NO COMPUTERS OR DIGITAL ENHANCEMENTS

No photo I have ever taken has entered a computer and come out a different photo. If there is an annoying power line in the shot I'll throw it away and try to get a clean shot on the next visit. This is a major point of pride for me. I want you to be assured that what you see is what was truly recorded on film.

NO COLOR FILTERS

During time-lapse photography Mother Nature will sometimes render her translucent aurora colors on film with an extra bold punch, especially on the red and violet ends of the spectrum where the human eye is the least sensitive. Some of this is due to extra color saturation occurring during a several second exposure, but I believe film is like an owl; it can see better at night than you or I can. This is all part of nature's art, as recorded on traditional 35 mm film. A color filter is just not needed.

NO DOUBLE EXPOSURES

Every shot is a single exposure. If a building or a tree appears lit up it is because I've used a spotlight or a hand-held flash for creative assistance with foreground lighting. I also use a penlight for "light writing." The shots that look like they were taken in the daytime can be attributed to moonlight, my favorite lighting of all. The moon acts as a huge natural flood lamp as it illuminates the snowscape below.

These are real "light show" experiences ~ as PURE as I can document them on film.

Index to photographs available as Limited Edition Prints:

www.AuroraHunter.com